SEO 2021 Ch...

Learn Search Engine Optimization

The 1-Page Success Plan:

Get New Customers, Make More Money, and Stand Out from the Crowd

Table of Content

On-Page SEO -- 6

Off-Page SEO ---6

Local SEO --7

Video SEO ---10

Why Your Work Needs SEO Services for Small Businesses? -----11

1. People are searching for you -- 11

2. It Pulls Quality Traffic ---12

3. More Chances of Getting Qualified Traffic -----------------------13

4. Increases Sales and Lead ---13

5. You Don't Need Paid Advertisements -----------------------------14

6. 24/7 Promotion of Your Business ---------------------------------14

7. It Influences Purchase Decisions ---------------------------------15

8. 90% More Clicks Than PPC --15

9. Increases Website Referrals --------------------------------------16

10. It Builds Trust and Credibility ----------------------------------17

What are Search Engines Actually Looking for? ----------------------17

First thing First – Relevancy ---18

Search Engines Care about Quality ----------------------------------18

Authority of the Website Matters ------------------------------------19

Meta Descriptions are Important for SEO ----------------------------19

It Doesn't Forget to Check Internal Linking ------------------------20

Why do You Need to Get SEO Services? -----------------------------20

Burning Your Pocket is terrible for Your Business -------------------21

SEO is an Ideal Solution for SEM Businesses ---------------------21

You Have Diversity of Information ------------------------------------22

Keep Track of the Performance --22

How to Ensure Expensive SEO is Better? -----------------------------23

How Do We Ensure Quality Services? --------------------------------23

White Hat Practices ---24

Guaranteed Quality ---24

100% Transparency ---24

An Eye on Trends ---24

Customer Satisfaction --24

Full SEO Solutions --25

SEO Marketing – It's a Necessity, Not Just an Option to Ignore -26

Why Local Brands Need Local SEO Services? ----------------------27

Local SEO Services that Really Work ---------------------------------29

1. Update Your Business Listings ------------------------------------29

   What Your Content Shouldn't Have ----------------------------32

2. Create Localized Content --34

3. Choose Your Keywords Smartly -----------------------------------35

4. Do Local Link Building ---38

5. Create Your 'Contact Us' Page Wisely ---------------------------39

7. Work on Your Website's Architecture ----------------------------43

8. Improve Dwell Time ---45

9. Use Local Keywords in Title Tags --------------------------------47

10. Mobile Optimization is Important --------------------------------48

Conclusion --49

SEO CHECKLIST --50

If you have any business that is present on the Internet, you should know what SEO (Search Engine Optimization) services are available and how they can help your business.

However, if you are not familiar with the concept in detail, don't worry.

This book will tell you everything you need to know to grow your business and improve your search engine rankings.

It's important to mention right from the start that SEO is something you can't do on your own.

You either need to hire a full-fledged SEO team or use SEO services.

Regardless of which option you choose, you should know that SEO doesn't have to be very expensive to be good. You can get affordable SEO services for small businesses and still achieve the results you want.

In this book, we've tried to tell you everything you need to know about SEO.

This will help you clarify your understanding of SEO, how it works, and why your business needs it.

I hope you get all your questions about search engine optimization and its benefits for your business answered.

So, without further ado, let's introduce you to what SEO is. Shall we?

What is SEO? – Everything You Need to Know

You may hear a lot of people say that you just need to add the right keywords and that will be enough to make your business stand out.

However, you should be aware that using keywords in your content will never work.

Google and other search engines have now developed their algorithms to prevent overuse of keywords.

Simply put, there are several ways to create an SEO and strategy, and you can also use all of the methods at the same time.

But, in order to know what affordable local small business SEO services you need, and what SEO goals you should set for your business, you need to understand the different types of SEO.

We have developed some of the very important SEO techniques to help you understand what SEO techniques your business needs to achieve the results you want.

Here you go:

On-Page SEO

An SEO practice that involves optimizing individual web pages for higher rankings and more traffic is called on-page SEO.

This will help you get more relevant search engine traffic.

It's important to note that on-page SEO refers to both the content and the HTML source of the page that can be optimized.

Here are some of the important on-page SEO key points to help you better understand this:

• Optimize URLs

• Includes keywords in heading tags.

• Format your copy

• Added alternative tags and images.

• Internal and external links are used

Off-Page SEO

If you think external SEO is just links, then you are wrong in many ways.

Off-page SEO is much deeper than that.

Unlike on-page SEO, you don't have complete control over your search engine optimization efforts. With external SEO, you need to reach out to bloggers and high domain authority websites to link you.

If you're still unsure about on-page and off-page SEO, ask yourself which SEO practice offers you more control.

If you don't have much control over this, then it's probably external SEO.

Here are some important features of out-of-page SEO:

• Requires an understanding of link building strategies.

• You must select more than one social platform to use

• You will need to conduct outreach to the community.

• You will need positive but honest reviews and ratings to build trust.

• You will need to reach out to influencers.

Local SEO

Affordable Local SEO Services for Small Business, as the name suggests, is an SEO strategy that is designed to improve your site's local search rankings. This means you can optimize your online presence to attract more business from local research.

Here's what local SEO can help you for your business:

• It allows your local customers to contact you.

• It helps to add structural location data to your site.

- It plays a vital role in optimizing Google My Business.

- It can help you check the mobile availability of your site.

Ecommerce SEO

When you search for something on Google, you are taken to a search engine results page (SERP).

There are different results that Google shows you.

This includes paid campaigns, sponsored purchases on Google, and the top ten organic searches.

Affordable ecommerce SEO services for small businesses are a guarantee that your product will make it to the top 10 of regular searches.

There are undoubtedly many pages that you can rank on.

However, you should be aware that the higher the page number on which you will rank, the less traffic will be.

This is how ecommerce SEO works:

- It helps to access the site architecture for ease of use.

- It helps you create content that meets the needs of your audience.

- This is the best way to optimize product listing on both Google and Amazon.

Technical SEO

The optimization process that helps search engines crawl and index your site efficiently is known as technical SEO.

It is imperative to note that without affordable technical SEO services for small businesses, you cannot change anything unless you focus on technical SEO.

This is why technical SEO is so important and you cannot ignore it:

• It helps in evaluating the structure of URLs.

• This helps to ensure that your site's navigation structure is logical and meaningful.

• Checks conical URLs

• It plays an important role in creating your 404 page.

• Provides more security for your site by adding SSL

• The absolute way to add your site to Google Search Console.

Video SEO

Affordable Small Business SEO Services Made Easy. All you have to do is optimize your video for indexing and ranking on search engine result pages for relevant keyword searches.

While many strategies can help, you should choose the one that best suits your business requirements.

Here's the process of optimizing your video for SEO purposes in a simple and effective way.

• You need to add video tags and description along with the video that you upload.

• Make sure you choose attractive and eye-catching icons for your video.

• Finally, you will need to set up your YouTube channel.

Now that you know about almost all types of SEO and how they work, it's time to understand why SEO is important to your business and why you need to hire affordable video SEO services.

Here's everything and anything you need to learn and know about it:

Why Your Work Needs SEO Services for Small Businesses?

When you own a business of any kind, you should think twice before making any decision about your business.

It's the same with choosing SEO for your business.

You have to ask yourself why your business needs this, and if you are already thinking about it, here's what you need to know about why your business needs SEO services:

Before we move ahead and tell you about the importance of SEO in the following paragraphs, it is important to note that this is not a complete list.

There are many more SEO benefits that it can offer your business.

So let's dive in and find out how you can improve your business with SEO:

1. People are searching for you

One of the most important things you need to know is that people are looking for the product you are selling online.

Hence, you need to be sure that when they search for a product or service that is relevant to your business, you will be put into research.

This will help them know that you exist and they will know that they have new and better opportunities to shop and do business.

But the real question is how to do it?

The answer lies in an effective SEO strategy.

A good affordable SEO and marketing services strategy will help you make sure that whenever someone searches for a product you are selling, your site will appear in front of them.

2. It Pulls Quality Traffic
If your goal is to rank high on the search engine, then you need to pull out a lot of threads at once.

One of these streams is the return of quality traffic to your website.

Almost all search engines recognize the increase in traffic to your site and increase the ranking of your site accordingly.

SEO plays a very important role in driving quality traffic to your website.

So, if you want more and more people to come to your site, you need to develop an effective SEO strategy.

3. More Chances of Getting Qualified Traffic

Driving traffic to your website isn't the only thing that will help your business.

If you want your business to take full advantage of the local SEO services available, you need to ensure that the traffic you receive is qualified.

This means that you will need to target specific audiences that can convert.

Simply put; you need convertible traffic to visit your website.

The good news is that you don't have to do much with it, and you just don't have to send people door to door to ask to do business with you.

We don't live in the 70s anymore. All you have to do is design an effective SEO campaign targeting a specific audience and this is how you will get more leads.

4. Increases Sales and Lead

In addition to getting qualified leads, you need to focus on increasing sales and retaining your current leads.

And, if your SEO strategy is not helping you increase sales and leads, you should take that as a hint and make changes to your SEO strategy.

A good and affordable SEO and search engine marketing strategy must be scalable and produce visible results.

It's clear that you can't see SEO results right away.

However, when you start implementing an effective SEO strategy, you start to see indicators that show whether you are heading in the right direction or not.

5. You Don't Need Paid Advertisements
If you're in luck with paid ads on Google and other social media, then it's time for you to reconsider your choice.

In any case, we are not saying that paid advertising is bad. But you need to know that you need a long-term advertising solution for your business.

Search engine optimization isn't free either, but you can always take advantage of the professional SEO services available and save money by using the affordable small business SEO packages.

If you want to continue your paid ad campaign, there is nothing wrong with that, but sooner or later you will have to think about a long-term solution for your company. Good for you, SEO can help.

6. 24/7 Promotion of Your Business
By paying for ads, you can reach your target audience within a limited period of time.

On the other hand, when you start uploading SEO content to your website or via guest posts, it stays online the entire time until you delete it yourself.

Thus, this means that your content will always be available to your potential customers.

Thus, you will practically be advertising your business 24 hours a day, 7 days a week, which is also less money.

7. It Influences Purchase Decisions

Done right, the small business SEO services available can help you influence your prospect's decision and they may end up buying from you.

What's more, you can create a positive story about your brand and influence your customers' buying decisions.

All you have to do is make sure that the content you use in your SEO strategy is engaging enough to turn your potential customers into real customers.

8. 90% More Clicks Than PPC

Did you know that a well-written, quality blog will get about 90% more clicks than any type of PPC advertising?

Pretty shocking, isn't it? The reason is pretty simple.

People are annoyed by ads and do not want to be distracted by ads when they do something important. And in their free time, they don't want to spend it watching ads.

Therefore, they just install ad blockers in their browsers, and the ads that you paid a lot of money for never reach their intended audience.

On the contrary, you can grab a lot of potential customer attention simply by making a headline that interests you.

The more interesting the topic and name of the blog, the more clicks there will be.

First of all, you can actually bring the reader back to your website by creating high quality content that grabs your reader's attention and makes them want to read more.

9. Increases Website Referrals
One of the most important benefits of affordable SEO services for websites is that they increase the number of conversions to websites.

By implementing the right SEO strategy, you will be able to attract more referrals to your website.

First of all, there is a high probability that your visitors will direct your site to their friends. However, for this to happen, you must ensure that a reasonable number of people are visiting your site.

10. It Builds Trust and Credibility

And finally, gaining the trust and credibility of your business is a major business requirement these days.

When a user sees your page or website in the top of Google or other search engines, they subconsciously begin to trust your brand. First of all, they tend to buy from brands that are in the top rankings.

So, in simple terms, if you want your potential customers to become your loyal customers, you need to make SEO your friend and build the trust they are looking for.

What are Search Engines Actually Looking for?

Throughout this article, we've said more than once that you need the right SEO strategy.

You must be wondering what the correct view actually is.

Basically, a good affordable search engine optimization strategy focuses on all aspects that a search engine is looking for.

Simply put, search engines operate according to a specific algorithm that continues to evolve and change over time.

An SEO strategy that meets all the requirements of a search engine for ranking content is a good SEO strategy.

To give you a detailed insight, here are some of the important things that search engines look for when ranking content.

First thing First – Relevancy

The first and most important thing is that search engines look for its relevance.

If your content is irrelevant to your business, and you are still uploading it after you hammered keywords into it, then you may not publish it at all.

It is important that you take content relevance into account when posting content, because that is the first thing a search engine looks for.

Search Engines Care about Quality

If you think the quality of the content doesn't matter because Google or other search engines aren't going to read it, then you are wrong.

If anything, almost all search engines prefer to rank quality and unique content over poorly written content.

So, make sure that any content you write for both internal and 0-page SEO is of great quality and must be 100% unique.

Authority of the Website Matters

If you are doing off-site search engine optimization, this means that you need to select sites with high domain authority to get the results you want.

If your content is published on low DA sites, it may not do any good to your business, and you may be spending money on affordable SEO and small business marketing services for your SEO strategy.

Meta Descriptions are Important for SEO

Not adding is one of the most common mistakes companies make when implementing their SEO strategies.

You should be aware that search engines are looking for meta descriptions of your content.

So, if you're not adding any meta tags, then it's time to fix that and start adding meta descriptions and get the most out of your SEO strategy.

Life of the Content is Vital

If you upload or publish content that will become irrelevant over time, this is really bad for your SEO strategy.

You must create content that will remain relevant to your readers and users for a long time. This is important because if the content has a short lifespan, people will stop seeing it, and therefore, you won't have new leads.

It Doesn't Forget to Check Internal Linking

When it comes to on-page SEO, it's very important not to forget about internal links.

Even with external SEO, internal links play a huge role.

So, you need to make sure you link to the internal pages of your site.

This will help you improve your search engine rankings and your SEO strategy will be more fruitful and yield long-term results.

Why do You Need to Get SEO Services?

If you've come this far in your book, then you already know everything you need to know about SEO.

Therefore, it is time to look for the options that you have to get an SEO service for your business.

When you go online and look for SEO services, you see all sorts of options popping up on the search engine.

The selection can become difficult to chew on the cookie. So, if you have doubts about choosing affordable small business SEO OR affordable small business SEO services, then don't overdo it and just do it.

Here are the reasons why you should choose affordable SEO services:

Burning Your Pocket is terrible for Your Business

When it comes to your business, maximizing your profits and savings is the ultimate goal of any business owner.

This is the reason why you have to be very careful when making money-related decisions.

So, if you want to save money and at the same time get reliable SEO services, then choosing the SEO services available is the right decision for your business.

SEO is an Ideal Solution for SEM Businesses

There are undoubtedly many big companies out there that spend fortunes on their SEO strategies.

They spend a lot of money on SEO because they have huge incomes and reserves and can afford it.

However, when it comes to small and medium businesses, this is not the case.

You have limited resources and need to make something useful out of them.

Therefore, choosing organic SEO services for small businesses is the best option for small and medium sized businesses globally.

You Have Diversity of Information

If you think that choosing an affordable SEO service company may not bring the results you want, then you are wrong in many ways.

There are many SEO consulting service providers available that have a huge variety of information when it comes to providing quality SEO services.

This way, you really don't need to worry about the quality of the service if you choose the right company.

Keep Track of the Performance

Another important thing about SEO is tracking the effectiveness of your SEO activity.

This will help you make the appropriate adjustments to your strategy. So, if you are receiving services from a reliable and authentic company, you do not need to worry about tracking your performance, because we will take care of it for you.

How to Ensure Expensive SEO is Better?

While choosing the best priced SEO services is a wise decision, if you still want to use expensive SEO services, you need to be sure that they are worth it and better than the rest.

But the real question is how to make sure expensive SEO is best for your business.

Here are some of the most important things you should check before hiring expensive SEO services:

• Ask them for their portfolios and examples of their previous clients.

• Ask them about the experience they have in this area.

• You should know a summary of their workflow

• Make sure you clearly state the time it will take for them to show results.

• Compare the additional services they provide with the SEO services available.

How Do We Ensure Quality Services?

Try your best to use the best and most effective SEO techniques that will provide the desired results for our clients and therefore improve their business:

Here's how we do it:

White Hat Practices
Our company is only focused on providing reliable services without any gimmicks or other tricky ways.

Guaranteed Quality
Quality has made us who we are today. Therefore, there can be no question of a compromise for us regarding the quality of our content and the sites selected.

100% Transparency
Our company keeps clients informed every step of the way. Our dashboard helps you seamlessly track the entire process in real time.

An Eye on Trends
Our dedicated team always keeps an eye on the changing dynamics of the SEO world to offer only the safest and most effective solutions.

Customer Satisfaction
Customer satisfaction is our satisfaction. We develop strategies and implement rigorous quality assurance procedures to deliver only the best.

Full SEO Solutions

It doesn't matter what kind of SEO services you are looking for, we provide you with a wide range of SEO services that we offer for your business.

Here is a list of SEO services that we offer to your business.

• Safe backlinks

• Detailed analysis of keywords

• Backlink analysis

• SEO audit services

• Increasing the authority of the site

• Testing the landing page

• Optimization of local maps

• Review of ratings and potential customers

• Regular fine tuning

* **Note:** this is not a complete list. We can offer many other SEO services as well. Contact us and let us know what services you want for your business.

SEO Marketing – It's a Necessity, Not Just an Option to Ignore

Whoever started calling Google algorithms by animal names, I'm pretty sure of one thing:

The clever leader of this mess knew that the online world would become a zoo in the coming years.

The penguin, panda, hummingbird and many more (you never know the panther is now being created at Google headquarters!) Will become the masters of this zoo, and brands will fight to become the king of the online world.

And it happens!

Brands are competing to rank at the top of the SERPs because this is no longer just an option.

What for?

Because:

All cherries go to the top sites.

The top 3 search rankings get 36% CTR, and 75% of search engines only stick to the first page of search results.

What does it mean?

SEO marketing is essential for your business.

Because it gives you:

- Search visibility

- Brand recognition

- Brand authority

- More potential customers

- Higher return on investment

As well as:

INCREASES CONVERSION!

Yes, you heard right.

The right SEO marketing tactics can help you with this.

And this is important not only for major global brands.

Local brands also need local SEO services to transform their bottom line.

Why Local Brands Need Local SEO Services?

If you didn't know before, now is the time to find out that local SEO is a thing and your local business needs it.

Not sure why?

Here's your answer:

Suppose you ...

Local bakery.

Nearby is a hairdresser.

Home service providers.

Car insurance company.

I'm sure you don't expect someone to come from the Middle East to get a haircut at your beauty salon located in Dallas or, say, Chicago.

Obviously, you want your local target customers to know about your business, visit your website or local store, and turn into your customers.

This is why you need local SEO services because there is a twist in the story.

Google's local SEO algorithms work on very different foundations than SEO for global websites.

So, you need to come up with a localized approach to SEO marketing.

Thanks to Google's Possum update, you need to seriously focus on local SEO more than ever before if you want to win the local search game.

It is difficult, we all know it, but not impossible.

Here are some tips and tricks that you can use in your local SEO marketing that will increase your conversion rate HUGE.

Local SEO Services that Really Work

1. Update Your Business Listings
Forget about backlinks and all other ranking factors.

First:

Google needs to know that your local business exists in the online world in order to rate you.

Business data will help you with this: you can register, find and get recognized on Google.

If you don't know

You might be wondering why you need this when you have a website.

Well, to understand, you need to take a step back and think about the offline marketing days.

You had a physical office, right?

But you still got into the Yellow Pages - those heavy business directories - remember?

What for? Because it was a marketing tactic.

Yesterday's Yellow Pages are today's listings of companies on the Internet.

The yellow pages were optional; local business lists - no.

They are an integral part of local SEO services.

Because listing helps:

- Build a solid reputation.

- Build trust and credibility.

- Make your business more searchable.

- Rating upgrade.

- Increase your income.

Bottom line?

Finding company information is essential to your local SEO.

Here's an example.

I was looking in New York for a coffee brand with the exact name "Plowshares Coffee Roasters".

It was listed on Google My Business listings, so it appeared in search results like this:

But what should you add when listing?

Is it enough to add your name, phone number and address?

The answer is no.

Try to add as much **accurate** and **up-to-date** information as possible on the website.

Said it was like your portfolio, and you don't give your portfolio to anyone without the necessary information.

So it's always best to add:

- Company name

- Address

- Phone number

- Tagline

- Logo

- Website URL

- Categories

- Description of services

- Social profiles

- Images

- Certificates

This will not only increase your credibility, but it will also provide the user with detailed information about your business.

But you just can't open a listing site and start typing in your company information.

Always Add Information Carefully

Google has a complete guide that you must follow to get listed in order to get the best results.

Based on these guidelines, we can clearly state that your information should be:

• Accurate

• Consistent

• Accurate

• To point

So always add information carefully because it will have a HUGE impact.

What Your Content Shouldn't Have
Now we talked about what you should add.

Then we'll talk about what shouldn't go into your content.

Yes, Google has guidelines for this.

• **Do not be misleading** by providing false, inaccurate or misleading information.

• **Do not create low-quality content** with poor readability, misspellings, mistakes and gimmicks.

• **Do not mention your promotions**, sales, or any other promotional content.

• **Never post links** in your content.

• **Do not display obscene, vulgar, offensive, terrorizing** or any other inappropriate concept in your content.

This means that you should refrain from adding any content that conflicts with the parameters of quality, correctness and honesty.

Choose the Right Listing Site

There are many catalogs, indexes, and business listing applications.

But not every platform is worth your time.

Choose the platform that can give you the best results carefully.

Initially, it's best to choose major platforms like Google My Business, Yelp, Bing Places, Yahoo, etc.

Monitor Your Profile and Update Changes

Change your profile as your business changes.

• If you changed your location, update the new address.

• If you have remodeled your workplace, upload new photos.

• If you have changed the opening-closing time, be sure to indicate it.

The reason is simple:

The list of companies is needed not only to improve the rating. It is also a source of great user experience.

So, if you add value to your customers, you have a chance to surpass the big business and be prominent on the listings.

This will help you draw more attention to your business.

2. Create Localized Content
Content is still king. And its value to Google is growing every day.

So the type of content you create for your SEO marketing matters a lot.

Since Google launched the Rank Brain algorithm, it has become much smarter at learning and understanding your content in order to provide better quality and most relevant search results to search engines.

It simply means that if you are a local travel company in Las Angeles, you cannot count on being ranked in the local search rankings if your website talks about the beauty of the Maldives.

You must create content with a local approach.

Here's an example.

This is the Toronto home maintenance provider website that appeared in the search results because I used the keyword Toronto Home Maintenance Services.

You can see that they used a localized approach throughout their content.

How?

• Specially reaching out to local audiences

• Keeping content for a specific niche

• Mentioning a specific city name more than a few times

This is what you should also do if you want to improve your rankings and increase your conversion rates.

3. Choose Your Keywords Smartly
Choosing the right keywords is one of the most important parts of a local SEO service.

People use keywords to find you, and Google uses those keywords to determine if you should appear in search results or not.

In short, keywords are like signs that people use to navigate to your site.

If you don't use a signage, your potential customers will land on someone else's website.

And you don't want that to happen.

This is why you need to know how your local users are looking for you.

Here are some tricks that can help you:

Ask Google

What's better than asking Google what keywords your potential customers are using to find you?

Nothing, right?

Obviously, no one knows this better than Google.

And it's very easy, because Google is always ready to give you keywords and search phrases.

For example, enter your primary keyword and scroll down.

Explosion!

In the middle of the page, Google gives you the search phrases that people use related to your keyword.

Amazing, isn't it?

But wait, the best is yet to come.

This gives you a clear idea of what long tail keywords and phrases users are using that you should be using in your content to boost your rankings.

Spy on Your Competitors

To be honest, we all love to know our competitors' secret recipe for success.

What if I said it was possible?

We may not be able to find the secret recipe for Coca-Cola.

But we can tell you exactly what keywords your competitors are using to increase their rankings.

Go to Ahrefs Site Explorer and enter your competitor's URL.

After that click on Organic Keywords and you will find the keywords your competitor is ranking for.

For example, I researched the URL of this site, which received a high ranking for the keyword Auto Insurance in Houston.

And I got everything.

• Keywords

• Volume

• Keyword density

• Position

Look like that's it!

The best thing about this is that you can easily find out which keywords are actually working.

In other words, you don't have to go through any tests and you can use proven keywords that can lead to real results.

4. Do Local Link Building

Today, backlinks are still one of the most important SEO factors to rank your website.

Google uses those backlinks as votes to determine the authority and credibility of your website.

The more backlinks you get from reputable sites, the higher your chances of ranking high in search results.

Unsurprisingly, many SEO professionals consider inbound link to be an important SEO factor.

This is why link building has long been a part of SEO marketing and continues to be an important practice.

But when you're going to create links for a local site, you need to start with a local mindset.

Getting links from influential global sites with global traffic isn't the best solution.

Because:

• Google will not count these votes for local rankings.

• Your brand awareness and credibility will not improve

• You will not receive targeted traffic

• You will not build relationships with local industry influencers.

In short, you won't get the benefits that we expect from our link building efforts.

Thus, for local SEO services, you should use links from specific niche, high quality local sites.

Here are some quick tips on how to get super effective, high-quality backlinks:

1. Create linkable resources on your site.

2. Conduct groundbreaking research work.

3. Create unique content that is difficult to find anywhere else.

4. Guest post on reputable sites.

5. Go to sites that link to your competitors.

6. Become an influencer in your industry.

This effort will move the needle for you.

You will start getting links from local authority sites and see dramatic positive changes in your local search rankings.

5. Create Your 'Contact Us' Page Wisely
It's so unfortunate that people pay little or no attention to it when they create their contact pages.

The Contact Us page isn't just for displaying the larger Request Quote form.

And this, too, is not to throw in multiple numbers, email addresses, and an incomplete address.

You have to make it as easy and simple as possible for search engines.

This will help a lot when people start looking for your location.

Here are few tips to make things easier for you:

Add Different Location Pages for Each Location

If your business is located in different locations, say one of your offices is in Chicago and the other in San Francisco, add different landing pages for them.

But your business may not get that kind of courtesy.

The problem is that when search engines crawl your site for indexing, they can get confused with so many URLs that fit on one page.

So create different landing pages for different places.

It will help people find your business and visit it easily without running into any obstacles.

Do I need to tell you that this will increase your conversion?

Add Your Contact Information Precisely

Google has tons of ranking options, so it doesn't have time to solve puzzles on your site.

It should return search results in seconds; anything that is confusing about your site can annoy Google.

Result? Your prospect may not find the contact information they need.

It's always best to choose your address once and for all and use it everywhere on the Internet.

For example, where are you going to use commas, abbreviations, etc.

Don't forget to add your sitemap as well, as it helps a lot with local SEO.

6. Get Google Reviews

Google reviews are more powerful than you think.

They can seriously make or break your business.

You can imagine the impact this would have on a potential buyer looking for a cool breakfast spot.

Think of the times when you wanted to consult a doctor, but did not know which one was better.

What did you do?

You've checked online reviews to find the best one.

If you nod right now, you are not alone. About 91% of consumers see online reviews.

What for? Because:

• People take online reviews as a personal recommendation.

• They increase the trust factor.

• They remove confusion and doubt.

• They facilitate decision making.

Therefore, ask your loyal customers to leave good reviews.

Once you start getting good reviews, it will have a positive effect on your CTR (click through rate).

Did you know that Google considers high CTRs to be a huge SEO factor?

Search intent is a new player in the SEO marketing world and Google attaches great importance to it.

Simply put:

You might be wondering what is the point of the answer to this question, because this is a search engine headache.

But remember that search engine is a Google headache because Google wants to give all of its search engines the best experience to stay on top.

As such, Google pays close attention to assessing whether a search result matches a search purpose.

How? By measuring your click-through rate.

When your site gets more clicks, Google considers that as a signal that it matches the search target.

Thus, it will increase your site's ranking.

As well as...? Increasing your search visibility will also increase your conversion rate.

The equation looks like this:

See? Getting positive reviews on Google can have a huge impact on your business.

Follow them.

7. Work on Your Website's Architecture
Website architecture is one of the most overlooked factors in local SEO services.

The architecture of a website is similar to the structure of a building.

Planning the floor plan...

How different rooms are arranged...

How the different sections are related...

Everything is important in the construction of a good building.

Similarly:

A website structure is the way an entire website is structured and linked.

The key is to give Google users and crawlers a seamless experience.

Here are some tips to help you improve the structure of your site:

• Build a simple structure; do not complicate the situation.

• If you have many pages, make categories.

• Do not place links only in the footer and header.

• Make internal links to give crawlers a route to index pages.

• Link relevant pages with exact match to the anchor text.

• Add a sitemap to make it easier for crawlers.

• Make the URL structure match the hierarchy.

It will work!

8. Improve Dwell Time

The head of Google Canada confirmed that Google uses timeout as an indicator for ranking a site.

Whether you are a global site or a local site, this rule remains the same for everyone.

This means that local SEO services should also focus on this SEO factor.

If you don't know what stay time is, here's what Wikipedia can tell you.

In short, latency is the amount of time a user spends on a website and Google started using it to rank the site.

Attracting a visitor to a website is one of the most important and difficult tasks for any website owner.

The problem is that consumer consumption patterns have changed.

They have so many options and little attention.

If your site doesn't appeal to them, they'll leave.

It is so simple.

Give Visitors What They Want

If you offer your visitors a user-friendly interface, they won't have a reason to go elsewhere.

This means giving your users what they want without much hassle.

For example, some websites report user problems without explicitly telling how they are going to solve them.

Listen: visitors already know about their problems.

They need solutions from you, so give them.

You can see that the solution is displayed right on the banner.

It definitely encourages visitors to scroll down to see how they're going to do it.

What does it mean?

The chances are that they will stay on your site and only go away after shopping.

Build Easy Navigation

Navigation on your website plays an important role in deciding whether visitors will stay on your site or not.

Google mentioned five common navigation mistakes in one of its blogs to avoid:

• **Mistake 1.** Using a non-standard location for navigation.

• **Mistake 2.** Using generic shortcuts for naming categories.

• **Mistake 3.** Using drop-down menus.

- **Mistake 4.** Rich navigation bar with too many options.

- **Mistake 5.** Wrong order of placing important things.

This means that if you can avoid these mistakes, you can greatly improve your navigation.

And better navigation means you give your visitors a good reason to stay on your site and help them find what they want.

Result?

Increased Chances of Conversion!

9. Use Local Keywords in Title Tags

Title tags and meta descriptions are important SEO factors on a website.

Your SEO website marketing efforts are useless without creating optimized title tags.

Google mainly uses title tags to understand what your site is about.

So using local keywords in your title tags gives you a free ticket to register with Google as a local website.

Nearly all search results use local keywords in title tags and meta descriptions.

This is what you should do too.

Watch out for even the smallest details, because the little things add up to a huge impact.

But keep in mind:

• Don't make it look like keyword stuffing.

• Make it natural

• Focus on providing value, not adding a keyword

Using local keywords in your title tag and meta description increases your chances of appearing in search results and being found by people.

So don't overlook this important local SEO factor.

10. Mobile Optimization is Important
We all know that mobile search is becoming popular.

People use mobile devices instead of computers to search, shop online, and browse websites.

For example, in the US in 2019, mobile search and spending was about $ 28.12 billion.

And the figure is not going to stop there. It will only increase.

This is why Google attaches great importance to responsive web design for ranking in order to give mobile users more experience.

When you find that 75% of local mobile searches result in an offline store visit within the first 24 hours, you can easily guess what you should be doing.

Make your site responsive to keep your customers and Google happy in a win-win situation.

Conclusion

The essence of getting SEO services for your business is that you will somehow improve the ranking of your business and improve sales.

So what are you waiting for? Contact us now and we will help you make your business better.

In today's tough online business environment, it is too difficult to increase conversions and increase revenue.

Having a website, great service, and great motivation will get you nowhere.

You need to move the envelope and do something to stir the scene.

Your website needs to rank first in the SERPs to grab customer attention and increase conversions.

But with SEO specialists, everything is too difficult.

And they get complicated when you are fighting for local SEO because things work differently here.

You must take a different approach to achieve the largest increase in your conversion rate.

But the good news is, it's possible.

Playing by the rules and following certain local SEO practices can go a long way.

Try them and let me know if they worked for you?

Let's see how local SEO marketing works magic for you!

Downloadable SEO CHECKLIST

The Google SEO Checklist is your step-by-step SEO framework that guides you through actionable strategies that you can use IMMEDIATELY to analyze, measure and improve the organic reach of any website in 2021.

Check it out and then go to File-> Make a Copy so you can make it yours

https://bit.ly/32CjB07